Contents

D1642364

Getting started...

Your checklist for a happy healthy pet

[ ] Dwarf Hamster cage
[ ] House or bedroom
[ ] Woodshavings
[ ] Dwarf Hamster bedding
[ ] Dwarf Hamster food
[ ] Food bowl
[ ] Water bottle
[ ] Mineral stone
[ ] Vitamin supplement
[ ] Bottle brush
[ ] Dwarf Hamster playball
[ ] Exercise wheel
[ ] Tubes & wooden toys
[ ] Gnawing sticks or chews
[ ] Dwarf Hamster treats
[ ] Cage disinfectant

Useful books

[✓] Good Pet Guide: The Dwarf Hamster
[ ] Pet Friendly: Dwarf Hamsters

Introduction

1. Dwarf Hamster

The dwarf hamster is a relatively new in the pet keeping world when compared to their other furry counterparts.

The *Russian Campbell's* hamster, *Russian* and *Winter white* hamster have only been bred and kept as pets since the early 1970s, '80s and '90s, though the species has been recognized ever since the end of the 1800s.

The dwarf hamster species can be broken into 5 breed types; **Russian**, **Russian winter white**, **Campbell's Russian**, **Roborovski's** hamster and the **Chinese hamster** *(although the Chinese hamster is not a true dwarf hamster and is more related to the genus of mice and rats).*

Due to its small size the dwarf hamster is more suited to older keepers. The *Roborovski's* hamster in particular, is agile, very fast, and can be challenging for young hands to keep hold of. The diet of dwarf hamsters is also slightly different to that of their larger *Syrian* cousins *(p10).*

Your new hamsters will provide you with plenty of fun as they play with each other and thoroughly enjoy climbing on and inside tunnels, exploring their home and toys.

Dwarf hamsters are normally very social pets and especially with their own kind, but it is important to raise them together from pups. They will normally reject the introduction of a hamster from an outside group.

Hamsters unlike some other rodents are generally odorless themselves but their cage will need cleaning out once a week to keep your little pet happy and fresh. They are a great all round pet and given the correct treatment *(as outlined in this book),* in a loving environment, they will thrive and make a great addition to the family.

"Did you know: A group of dwarf hamsters is called a 'Clutch'?"

2. Origins & habitat

Campbell's Russian & Russian hamsters: *(Phodopus Campbelli)* Dwarf hamsters originate from the desert ranges of Asia, along the Russia/ Mongolia borders. They where first catalogued around 1905 by W.C. Campbell, who discovered them in Tuva, Russia, but they are also found in Northern China and central Asia. They dig deep borrows of up to 3 feet and line them with wool gathered from surrounding herd planes. First breed as a pet in 1973 in the U.K and then imported to the U.S. in the late '80s.

Roborovski's Hamster: *(Phodopus Roborovski)* First discovered in 1894 by Lt Vsevolod Roborovski while traveling across the Gobi desert. They are very efficient with their consumption of water and like the *Campbell's* hamster, they enjoy the security of borrows and this desire should be encouraged as pets. The original breeding family of the *Robo (as it's commonly called)* came from Holland in 1990.

Winter White: *(Phodopus Sungorus)* These pretty looking dwarfs where first classified as a coat variation of the *Campbell's Russian*, however, recent research into the breeds has shown that this is a misclassification and that it is a different species of dwarf hamster all together. This species have the unique ability to change their coloration in accordance to season. They are most commonly found in Siberia and Kazakhstan where they inhabit grassy hillsides.

KAZAKHSTAN, N. CHINA
SIBERIA MONGOLIA & RUSSIA

Top tips

Chinese hamsters:

(Cricetulus Griseus - Meaning rat like). Found in North China and Mongolia. Little is known as to the first classification of these rodents, however it is known that Professor Israel Aharoni *(of Syrian hamster fame)* was the first to document them fully in 1930. The *Chinese* hamster because of a misclassification is actually more related to the genus of the mouse and rat.

✔

3. Life span

Dwarf hamsters have a quite short lifespan when compared to their *Syrian* cousins living between 12 to 18 months on average.

When choosing your dwarf hamster ensure that it is at least 6 to 8 weeks of age so that you can be sure that they have been weaned fully and are eating well. If you buy your pet at an early age, you'll have the benefit of being able to enjoy you hamster for longer and if it's handled lovingly from an early age they will certainly be more friendly and relaxed around their human friends.

Perfect pet?

4. Great pets

Hamster world records

Oldest hamster world record :
7 years

Longest hamster (*Syrian*):
up to 34 cm *(about 13.5 inches)*

High Jump world record:
20 cm *(7.8 in)* Sweden 16 Mar '03.

Your hamster will greatly enjoy exploring their habitats. They are generally happy, inquisitive & lively little pets during the early evening. This is one of the reasons why the hamster is one of the most popular pets throughout the world.

Hamsters make especially good pets for those at work or school during the day. They are less active during the daytime and provided they are given sufficiently quiet housing *(out of direct sunlight)* they will sleep throughout the day, only waking to have the occasional snack from their food store or drink from their water bottle. Hamsters are fun to handle, but only for a short period, any longer and they will become anxious and will want to seek refuge in their cage.

A tame hamster will eagerly take a healthy treat from their human friends' fingers and quickly pouch this tasty morsel to be enjoyed later.

Many people enjoy watching their hamster explore the house by placing them into a hamster ball, this is a great way for your hamster to stretch their legs and satisfy their natural curiosity. However, be careful of any other animals around and also make sure the lid is on securely as a hamster will quickly escape if this falls off!

5. One or more?

Dwarf hamsters, unlike the *Syrian*, enjoy the security offered by having friends around them.

They will usually get along fine, but be prepared for the possibility of separating your hamsters should they fall out. You should never house odd numbers of dwarf hamster as this rarely works out and one will always fall out of the rest and as a result will be isolated, depressed and often bullied.

In order to keep equilibrium amongst the ranks provide a house, a water bottle, wheel and food bowl for each of the cage mates and a universal play area for all of them to meet and play.

Varieties

There are three varieties of Dwarf Russian hamsters:

6. Campbell's Russian

The body shape retains the same body shape as that of the *Russian dwarf*. They have hair on their feet and a slightly thicker coat that can be in a variation of colors such as mottled black, brown, grey or rarely, white with orange tips. All coats still retain the darker dorsal line and white belly pattern.

7. Roborovski *(often called 'Robo')*

The smallest of the dwarf hamsters and by far the fastest.

These adorable and cute faced hamsters are characterized by their brown flecked back and face, white belly, flanks and white eyebrows. They have a round flexible body and a lively disposition reaching 3 inches (7.4 cm) when fully grown.

8. Winter White

Similar in size and body shape as the Campbell's Russian, but their grey coloration is a little lighter in shade and depth.

This breed is characterised by their ability to alter their coat colors to a very light grey or even bright snow white. This color change is triggered by seasonal day length around the autumn and winter months. Other variations have been bred, such as the orange flecked or pink tinge coat, although these are rare and not often found in pet shops.

9. Chinese

Although often called a Dwarf Hamster, the Chinese hamster is actually from a group known as 'rat-like' hamsters. They have a tail of around 1.5 inches (3.8 cm) that is both flexible and useful.

It shows their family roots are firmly in the mouse and rat family, rather than hamster. Their bodies are characterized by their lean structure, perfectly designed for the flexible movements needed to climb the long grasses of their natural terrain. They only reach a size of 3 inches (7.4 cm) when fully grown and have a gentle and pleasant nature that cling lovingly to their handlers' fingers during cuddle time. Normally fully grey bodied, lighter bellies and with a dark, almost black dorsal line running the length of their back, but white flanked varieties are becoming more common.

Top tips

Hamster pouches

Hamsters pouches are so large and flexible that they can squeeze roughly half of their body size worth of food and treats into them!

Fun fact

The name *hamster* comes from the German word *'hamstern'* meaning *'to horde'*

Your dwarf hamster

10. Male or female?

It can be quite difficult to tell the sex of a young *'pup'* hamsters, if you have any doubts, the store staff can confirm your hamsters sex for you *(the pictures and instructions below should help when you are sexing your hamster).*

Male *Chinese* hamsters again show their rat and mouse relatives roots by presenting a very large fat filled scrotum that is almost a third of their own body size. This can make them look rather unappealing, so females tend to be more popular with many pet purchasers.

Top tips

Pet shop

Even pet shop owners can make mistakes with the sex of hamsters so it is usually a good idea to have a double check yourself before purchasing. ✓

The left shows the male while the right shows the female. Notice that on the male, the space between the penis and anus is further apart that the urethra and anus of the female, notice also the small hole close to the urethra, this is the hamsters vagina. Once the males reach a level of sexual maturity, around 4 to 6 weeks the testicles descend, giving the male hamster their typical almond shaped rump, as opposed to the females rounded rump.

Male   Female

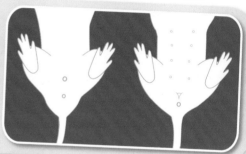

11. Choosing your hamster

Ensure that the pet you choose is active and interested in its surroundings has a clean well groomed coat, clean ears, bright eyes, and a well formed body free of scabs, lumps, bald patches and signs of wounds. **Below are a few things to consider when choosing your dwarf hamster**

→ Mouth

Your hamster should show no signs of dribbling or scabbing at the corners of the mouth, this could be a sign of infection through fighting, poor health, or teeth problems.

→ Eyes

Should be bright and alert with no sign of discharge or cloudiness. If they look dull it could be sign of a more serious health issue, check regularly for foreign bodies.

→ Ears

A hamsters hearing is much better than ours. Their ears are nearly hairless, and held upright and alert. When first woken, a hamsters ears are folded and flat, so allow time for them to extend their ears before handling. A small amount of wax inside the ear is perfectly normal, but if more than this is present it should be cleaned out.

→ Teeth

As with all rodents, a hamsters teeth constantly grow 16 teeth, 2 upper incisors, 2 lower incisors and 3 molars on each jaw, upper and lower. The teeth of a hamster should have a yellow tinge to them *(this denotes health)*. If the hamsters teeth are a bright white, there could be an underlying health issue, or poor diet.

→ Tail

The tail of a dwarf hamster is quite short with the exception of the *Chinese* hamster who's tail is around one inch in length. It should be clean and flexible, and show no signs of breakage or discharge around the base.

→ Paws

The dwarf hamster *(except the Campbell's)* has hairless feet with each front paw having four toes, and the back paw has five. Ensure that the individual toes are straight and supple and the nails do not under tuck or jut to the side.

→ Hiding

A hamster when first woken will most likely want to know what is going on and may be a little grumpy, allow them to wake up fully. Once awake however, they may run to seek refuge in their bolt hole, this is normal behavior and signifies that it is fit and healthy. Because hamsters are what is termed *hunted animals* this is a natural response to a possible predator.

→ Hair

If the hair around the hamsters rump is matted, it could mean the hamster is suffering from diarrhoea or 'wet tail' as it is most commonly referred to with hamsters. The coat should have a glossy coat with no bald patches and obviously well kept by the hamster.

→ Attitude/ personality

A hamster once awakened should show a normal inquisitive posture *(not hunched or curled)*, have a healthy appetite and sharp, lively reactions *(a lethargic hamster is one may be unhealthy)*.

→ Nose

Make sure the nose is clean, there shouldn't be any mucus in or around the nose.

Housing dwarf hamsters

12. Cages

By far the most popular type of habitat for hamsters is one made of wire. When choosing a suitable home for your dwarf hamster, you must make sure that it provides, not only a suitable environment for it to live comfortably, but also prevents its escape.

1.

Hamsters are very active little animals and therefore require stimulation and space to play. If a cage is too small, they will become bored and antisocial, leading to unpleasant behavioral traits, such as biting and bar gnawing and fighting with each other. The cage you choose must have enough floor space to allow your pets their own area, each should have their own wheel, food bowl and water bottle. Many people build their own cages out of plastic storage containers. These are called *'bin cages'*, and even though they are fiddly to construct *(adult supervision advised)*, they are as much fun to create as they are for your hamsters to enjoy.

A major consideration for your cage should be how far apart the bars are. A good rule to remember is, if you can fit your index finger through the bars then a dwarf hamster can squeeze through. Therefore, many of the cages for a *Syrian* hamster are not suitable. However, a good range of cages are available that are specifically designed for dwarfs.

13. Aquarium/ plastic cages

There are many plastic cages or glass aquariums available for dwarf hamsters. The *robo* is better kept in glass or plastic style enclosures because they can flatten themselves to no more than 0.75 cm in height and are sure to escape from the most secure of cages.

2.

One thing to remember is that an all enclosed habitat will require very regular cleaning *(around once every 3 days)*, and more often in the warmer months. Room for climbing and reaching toys must be given to your little friends because there are no bars for them to climb and explore.

This type of enclosure also has restricted ventilation and can be harder to clean. Silicon on some older fish tanks are toxic to small animals as they may have traces of fungicides that contain arsenic. For this reason it is worth making sure that you purchase an animal safe style tank you'll find that newer aquariums don't have this toxic silicon.

14. Introducing the cage

Ideally your new pets home should be already set up before purchasing your pets.

Ask the assistant to place some of their existing bedding and put both of the hamsters you choose into the travel box. This will make your pets more comfortable on the way home and will help them to relax once they are in their new home, as their scent is already present on the bedding upon introduction. You should never remove the hamsters from their travel box. Allow your hamsters to explore their new home on their own.

Let them roam freely to begin with to explore their new surroundings. Try not to pick your new pets up for a few days to let them become accustomed to their new home and you. Speak softly to your hamsters and use their names frequently.

Once they are used to their new home, be careful to acclimatize them to human contact slowly. Start by stroking your hamsters with one finger while they are roaming. Next, rub a little of their shavings in your hands, to scent your hands, then place a treat onto you palm, allowing your hamsters to wander onto your hand to retrieve it. Do not rush this and If you hamster does not want to be picked up yet, respect this and allow them to wander off again to store this new treat. Repeat this until they stay on your hand. Gently lift your hamster out of the cage, speaking softly to them. Hold your hamster in the palm of you're hand and against your chest gently stroking them with one finger. Remember, if you treat one hamster, you must treat the other to avoid fighting and jealousy.

Top tips

Hidey holes

Hamsters love small spaces to squeeze through and relax in, *toilet tubes, plastic cube mazes, hamster houses* are all enjoyed greatly as these type of hiding place simulates the same feeling of security that they would have in their wild habitats.

All hamsters must have a hiding space in there cage *(this helps to satisfy their instinct to flee when they feel threatened)*, either a wooden hidey hole or hamster house made of grass or plastic will provide enough of a snug environment to make them feel safe. You must provide a hidey hole for each of the hamster group, other wise they may fight or fall out.

3.

1. Dwarf hamster suitable cage.
2. A small plastic cage.
3. A converted old fish tank.

Dwarf hamsters food guide

15. Food glorious food

All animals, like humans, have different tastes and what one hamster devours with relish, another will simply sniff at and walk away from. Get to know what your hamster enjoys and use this as a treat once you place them back into their cage to re-enforce that they have been good.

There are many food types to choose from, but you should never change foods to quickly from one brand to another as this can cause stomach upsets.

The most common staple diet for hamsters is in the form of muesli that contains all of the nutrients needed to keep your hamster healthy and happy. Hamster muesli is a complete food and contains all of the vitamins and proteins they need, including meat proteins such as chicken.

16. Good treat foods

As mentioned, dwarf hamsters are very sensitive to sugars so you must be careful when giving fresh treat foods to your little pets.

To be safe the only fresh food that should be given to them would be a small piece of broccoli each or a small piece of carrot. Once in a while a small piece of apple each will be eagerly taken. Avoid sweetcorn (*dried is acceptable*) and fruits rich in acids and sugars.

Hamsters, like humans are omnivores and would eat small grubs and insects in the wild, as well as seeds and roots. You must be aware that dwarf hamsters are very prone to diabetes (*p16*) so any foods that contains too much fruit and sugars must be avoided.

There are specialist dwarf hamster foods available that are perfectly balanced to meet your new pet's specific dietary needs.

1. Dwarf hamster muesli.
2. Dwarf hamster friendly wood mix.
3. Water bottle.

17. Treats

Other treats specifically designed for dwarf hamsters and degus are suitable and available through your local pet shop.

These include hanging stick treats, often made with nuts and seeds, animal chocolate drops as well as honey drops. Natural wood treat packs are greatly received and enjoyed to the fullest as they mimic the food they would forage for in the wild. It is certainly worth reading the ingredients of many treats as most contain honey or glucose. Other treats to avoid are animal chocolate drops, raisins and currant chocolate drops. Yogurt drops are fine but only in small doses.

Hamsters also enjoy the occasional piece o**f cooked chicken or beef.** But only in small amounts as this may cause diarrhoea and obesity if given to often and in too large a quantity.

18. Pellets

There are specially made from a pellet *(laboratory blocks)* or a biscuit.

The benefits of feeding pellet or biscuit food is that it not only helps keep your hamsters teeth in good condition and well worn, it also stops your pet from selective feeding.

Selective feeding is when your hamster only eats the parts of the food that they want to, quite often leaving the parts of food in the muesli that are of real benefit to them.

Important!

Hamsters are naturally drawn to water so if your pet escapes, try placing a small bowl of water inside a bucket, place a ladder up to the top and bedding in the bottom to try to catch them.

Top tips

Vitamin Supplement

There are several vitamin supplements that are available for your small animal.

These can be placed either directly into the water bottle with their water or sprinkled onto their food. This is not always necessary unless your hamster is feeling a little under the weather.

✔

19. Water

The amount of water your dwarf hamster needs will vary, so it is always advisable that you have a constant supply of water within easy reach of your pet.

The water should be available in a bottle as a bowl will quickly become soiled and unhealthy for you pet to drink. Mark the fill level of their water bottle and refresh daily. This lets you see how much your pet drinks, and if there are any changes in the quantity consumed.

Play time

20. Exercise

Hamsters are lively and energetic little animals and require a great deal of exercise to keep them in good condition and help them live a long healthy life.

In the wild, a hamster will run up to 5 miles a night in the search for food and water. This need to run is a compulsion your hamster still has and without the opportunity to express this natural instinct your hamster may become very lazy, sleep a lot more and become overweight and as a result, as with humans, hamsters can experience similar health problems that arise as a result of being overweight. If your pet gets overweight they will have higher tendencies for heart disease, diabetes, bladder infections, respiratory problems and joint conditions. A large cage with enough room to play and a hamster wheel can help keep your pet in good shape and ensure that they live a rich, healthy life.

Another great way to keep your hamster in good health and fit is to place them into a hamster ball, not only will this be great fun to watch, but a great way for your hamster to work off extra energy they have, as well as giving their little muscles a work out. Ensure your Dwarf Hamster is excersised for no more than 15 minutes at a time.

1.

21. Play

In their natural environment hamsters will play when they are young pups and continue to play fight and wrestle into adulthood.

In this play period they learn how to fight and to hunt as well as to compete for a dominant role within the group. When they reach adulthood they still retain this need to play and will enjoy this activity. They will still love to explore, work out puzzles, run and will greatly enjoy the affections of their fellow cage mates as well as their human friends.

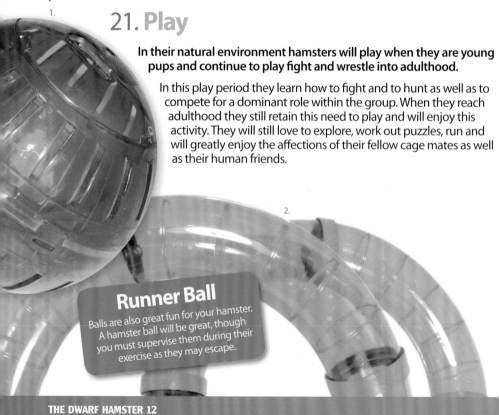

2.

Runner Ball
Balls are also great fun for your hamster. A hamster ball will be great, though you must supervise them during their exercise as they may escape.

22. Accessories

Different dwarf hamsters enjoy different types of toys but all enjoy the simple pleasure of running through cardboard mazes in the search for a tasty hidden treat, cardboard tubes and small cardboard boxes are great too. An exercise wheel is an essential item for all hamsters as are gnaw blocks and toys that they can drag around.

The best way to find your pets favorite is to simply experiment until you find a toy that entertains your particular pet. Usually the simpler the toy the better.

Some of the dwarf hamster favorites are:

A toilet paper tube | a medium sized cardboard box | willow balls | plastic animal ball with bell | hanging fruit wood toys | a straw basket | tubes | plastic extensions for cages | maze

Change the toys, houses, and locations of toys frequently to keep things fresh and interesting for your pet.

Keep toys, and especially houses and food dishes away from the walls and corners of the cage. Not only will they use a certain corner of the cage as their toilet but you will need to ensure that the walls of the cage are clear to allow them room to exercise *(they will use this space to run around the perimeter and to climb).*

1. Runner ball.
2. Plastic extension tubes.
3. Wooden log hidey hole.
4. Exercise wheel.
5. Sand bath.

NB. Syrians are likely to need an 8 inch wheel. If they don't use it, it could be because the wheel's too small.

Top tips

Sand bath

Once a week your pets would appreciate a sand bath using *chinchilla sand*, don't use *chinchilla dust* or a clay based sand as this can cause Irritation and lung problems.

Hamsters love to roll around in a bowl of this sand to wash their coats as it mimics their natural environments and bathing behaviors.

✔

Hamster grooming

23. Grooming

Grooming should be part of your daily play routine when handling your hamsters, even though they will groom each other.

This activity, will prove to be of great enjoyment for your hamsters but will also gives you an opportunity to perform health checks on your pets. As regular contact of this nature will offer you a greater insight into any changes in you hamsters body, coat conditions and can be of great help in spotting any indications of illness *(if you are unsure of anything that you find, consult your veterinarian)*.

Hamsters are very clean and tidy little animals and spend a great deal of their time grooming themselves and each other. They don't tend to molt in the traditional sense as their coat does not need changing as often as guinea pigs or rabbits.

To groom your hamster you will need a:

Brush: a soft bristle tooth brush is best.
Nail trimmer: Guillotine type or human kind can work as well *(pictured below)*.

24. Trimming nails

We recommend you take your pets to a vet or an experienced dwarf hamster keeper for nail trimming.

However, in time and with the relative experience you may find that you can do it yourself. Although, it is still advised that you first speak to a veterinary surgeon who can guide you through the technique of nail trimming.

On the whole, hamsters do tend to their own nails and the climbing and scratching they do while creating their little borrows in the shaving keeps them in good condition. However, as your hamster ages, the nails can grow faster than they are worn down by scratching and burrowing, so you may need to have them clipped.

It is important to note that there is part within the nail called the '*quick*' this vein is where the blood vessels and nerve endings are located. If you do accidently cut into the *quick* you will cause bleeding as well as considerable pain to you pet. The aim is to just clip just the sharp tip of the nail without damaging the *quick*.

1.

1. Rabbit friendly nail trimmer.

Health

25. Good health

To ensure your hamster remains in good health, make sure that their diet has an adequate intake of vitamins and minerals, through a balanced, complete and high quality diet that is very low in sugars.

26. Wood gnaws

Wood gnaws are available in pet shops or you can provide your own by supplying your hamster with a piece of unsprayed fruit branch or untreated wood block to gnaw on.

These will provide your pet with something on which to keep its teeth nice and trim. It would be a good idea to age the branches if you choose to use these, as the drying process is extremely important as some of these branches are poisonous while fresh.

Did you know?
Did you know the word 'rodent' is derived from the Latin word 'rodere' which means 'to gnaw'.

27. Health checks

Here are a couple of easy health checks that you can do yourself while you are grooming or playing with your pet.

Check through your hamsters coat by running the tip of your finger against the lay of the hair to see if there is any dry skin or bald spots which may be indicative of a fungal or parasitic skin condition. Check that its teeth are not broken, loose or over growing. Checks to see if the nose is dry, eyes are bright and that the hamsters' movements are decisive and they are curious about their surroundings *(see p7).*

28. Health problems

→ → Constipation and diarrhoea

This should be taken very seriously, they can be caused by a bad diet, illness or stress. *Consult a vet if you have any queries.*

→ → Respiratory infections

Hamsters are prone to respiratory infections and will usually have very similar symptoms to that of the human common cold.

However, it can be have a more serious impact on hamsters and should not be left untreated as it can lead to *pneumonia.* Keep out of damp, drafty environments and if the symptoms continue, consult your veterinarian for further advice.

Hamsters can catch a human cold or flu virus, so it is recommended that if you are ill with one of these you should avoid handling you pet until you are better.

→ → Diabetes

All too common with dwarf hamsters, and often over looked. **The signs are:** *frequent urination, a reluctance to eat, lethargy, rapid weight loss, diarrhoea, hunched posturing* and a *greasy coat.* The urine will often be very dark and have a strong smell and the stools loose and fluid. If you suspect diabetes you must take you little pet to a veterinary surgeon straight away. Take with you some of the urine soaked shavings, as this can help your vet to perform a diabetes test and insulin curve.

● ●

If you think one of your hamster is ill, take your pet to a qualified vet.

Top tips

Eye injuries

These are fairly common in dwarf hamsters. Usually caused by sharp objects or shavings flying into the eye while digging, exploring or falling while climbing.

A saline wash flush the eye of any foreign bodies but consult your vet if problems persist.

→ → Parasites

Scratching is a common symptom of a skin complaint often brought about by parasites like lice, mites and fleas.

Hamsters are usually free from parasites but if your pet gets an infestation, treat with a specialised medicated shampoo, mild insecticide powder or small animal 'Spot On' drop. If you have any queries, seek veterinary advice.

Cage care

29. Home sweet home

A covering is required for the floor of the cage to provide a soft, comfortable surface for your hamster to rest and feel comfortable on as well as to soak up the urine.

Dwarf hamsters require their substrate to be a little deeper than that of *Syrian* hamsters as they have an urge to borrow and dig, therefore a depth of around 5 inches (12.7 cm) is preferred. Fine sawdust should be avoided as this can cause irritation to the eyes and to the lungs.

Cedar wood shavings (*usually distinguished by a red tint*) should not be used as the *phenols* they contain can cause severe irritations in small animals. Although pine is also a softwood, **pine wood shavings** cause less problems than cedar and **kiln dried pine** can be used without problems.

You should steer clear of any scented shavings as these can cause irritation to your dwarf hamster and causes distress by masking their scent. Corn cob bedding is not generally recommended. It has a tendency to mould, and this can be eaten by your hamster or become trapped in their pouches and swell. Wood shavings from hardwoods such as aspen or small animal litter made from wood pulp are the safest forms of floor covering to use.

30. Cage cleaning

It has been said that hamsters are relatively odorless pets, However, even an odorless pets cage will start to smell if it is not cleaned for an extended period.

Urine soaked bedding and faeces and decaying vegetable matter all make your pets cage an unpleasant place to live and encourage flies and other pests to take hold.

→ Remove your hamster and make sure you place them in a safe and secure place before you begin cleaning. A plastic small animal carrier or small plastic tank is suitable.

→ Once a day you should remove all droppings and any uneaten fresh food. Ideally any fresh food given as a treat should be fed the night before your weekly clean.

→ Check that the bedding and cage litter is dry (*as damp conditions are very bad for small animals*).

→ Tidy the sleeping area and ensure that they have fresh clean water and the bottle is free of algae (*use a mild animal safe detergent once a week to clean the water bottle, rinse thoroughly and replace with fresh water in the hutch*).

→ Once a week, clean the whole cage using a brush and good animal-friendly cleaning disinfectant (*wait until the inside of the cage and base is completely dry before replacing the litter and bedding and putting hamster back in*).

Handling your hamster

31. Gently does it

Hamsters by nature are timid animals and will often shirk attention from you initially. However, if handled gently from an early age, they will soon become used to being picked up by you.

Initially, remember that you are much bigger than your hamster. Try not to reach down on top of your pet as their close range sight is very poor and it may think that you are a predator. In the wild hamsters are often hunted from above by birds of prey and your hand can easily be confused for one if you approach them from above.

You should first, rub some of their bedding in your hands to place their scent on you. Then softly stroke their head and back, hamsters do not like their cheeks or faces being touched so be careful.

Speak softly to your pet, using their name frequently and reassuringly. Place a favoured treat on the palm of your hand and lay it down back down flat against the cage base, and wait for you hamster to come to you. Once your hamster is comfortable retrieving the treat from your hand, you can move onto the next stage.

Next, wait until they are settled on and sniffing your hand, and gently your raise hand out of the cage, cupping your free hand around them to prevent them from falling or scuttling off as they are lifted. Keep them calm throughout the lifting process.

Talk gently to your hamster whilst gently stroking their back with your thumb. After you have gained their trust and they feel safe gently pull them into your chest and gently stroke their backs talking softly to them.

If you are new to hamsters then you should kneel down on the floor to lift them up, this will minimise the chance of any injury should your hamster wriggle free. They are fragile creatures and can suffer greatly if dropped, even if from a short heights.

32. Small children and safety

Children should be sat down *(preferably on the floor)*, **when you pass the hamster to them.**

Be prepared to remove the hamster if it becomes agitated as a child will sometimes struggle to keep a hold of a small animal and if they squeeze their pet to tight it may bite or worse, become injured through an accidental tight grasp.

Teach them to be gentle and to only stroke the hair in the direction the hair is growing.

When placing your hamster back in their cage, they can become quite excited, so be extra careful not to drop them. Try to release your hold on them only once they are safely on the ground.

33. Stroking

If your hamster is not in the mood for stroking they will let you know by turning their heads sharply toward you and raising their front paws, or they may *crackle* **at you.**

Never stroke a hamsters stomach as this is a sign of dominance and they become quite scared or bite.

34. Vocalizations

Hamsters are not particularly vocal little animals, making only the occasional squeak on rare occasions. Though one sound you may hear is *'Crackling'.*

→ Crackling

Sounds a little like an electric discharge. This sound is used to warn off predators or to show fear. If this sound is not heeded you may receive a rather nasty nip. If your hamster makes this noise as you approach, it is best to leave them alone until they calm down.

Top tips

Sociable

Dwarf hamsters are social, communal little creatures, enjoying the security of having others of their own kind around them, They should always be kept in even numbers to avoid bullying or victimization.

The group must be brought at the same time and preferably from the same *clutch*. The *Robo* hamster is a little less friendly toward humans and can be reluctant at being held and cuddled, but with care and perseverance they will soon look forward to your visits and treat foods. It is worth mentioning that even hamsters from the same clutch can fall out with each other once they become older, so it is advisable to have a spare cage in reserve for just this kind of event.

Know your dwarf hamster

35. Hamster anatomy

The anatomy of the hamster is the result of years of evolution and shows the adaptations it has had to undertake to survive.

Their body is designed for its main tasks, eating, reproducing and fleeing from predators.

Their heightened senses and ability to spot danger early and run for cover gave them an evolutionary edge and is the main reason that the rodent species has flourished where others have failed.

All hamsters posses the same physical features of a flat nose, short legs and very short tail.

36. Know your hamsters behavior

→ **Jumping**

Jumping straight up in the air is a typical display of joy.

→ **Sitting up**

Sitting up with their teeth bared in what looks like a smile with their paws held In front typically means back away I am about to bite.

→ **Rolling on to their backs**

Fear, submissive, offering of peace.

→ **Mouth wide open, showing teeth and crackling**

Vocal warning to predators.

→ **Stretching the head forwards and walking in jerks**

Watchful and alert.

→ **Retracting legs under body and backed up against a wall**

Helpless and scared, needing protection.

→ **Stress**

Stress will impact on your pets immune system and can adversely affect its ability to fight off infections.

Keep your hamster away from extreme temperatures and drafts, and away from intimidating animals/people. To relieve stress make sure your hamster has plenty of place in which to retreat if they feel threatened.

Breeding advice

37. Golden rules of breeding

Before even considering breeding hamsters, it is best to make sure that you can find homes for the inevitable litter.

The average litter of pups is between 6 to 12, it is also quiet common for a female dwarf to be re-inseminated while still pregnant. Unlike most other animals in the world, a female dwarf can hold the gestation period in a state of suspension while nursing her first litter, only to continue it once her pups have been weaned and removed from the nest.

You must never interfere with the mother when she has had her litter, she will see this interaction between you and her young as a threat and she may eat her pups. This is a response still held from the wild, where she will eat the pups to gain the energy she needs to run for a great distance to find a new home and escape danger.

After she has become pregnant you will find that her personality may change from being cute and gentle, seeking you're attention, to being guarded and aggressive. She becomes like this as she wants to be left alone to build her nest and raise her young. Do not try to hold her during this stage as she may bite or miscarry through stress. Just before she has her pups and while she is nursing them It Is of vital importance that you do not try to clean out her nest area, she will do this for you by throwing out any soiled bedding. Simply remove this and place fresh into the cage for her to take back into her nesting place.

The whole gestation and weaning period takes no longer than 45 days, but throughout this time the mother will need extra food and the addition of a *mineral stone* to her cage as well as extra vitamins in her water will be greatly appreciated.

38. Preparing the cage

Provide the mother with extra bedding and at least 2 houses or nesting areas, also she will need extra food and minerals in the form of a block.

A single layered cage is better though pups (born blind), do still tend to wander around after about 4 days and can easily become lost and disorientated. Make sure that the water bottle is at a reachable height for the young arrivals and that food is easily accessible to them for when they begin to eat solids. It is a good idea to have enough space outside of the nesting area for the mother to toss soiled bedding for you to collect and fresh to be placed, with as little interaction as possible from yourself.

39. Introductions

With the exception of the *Chinese* hamster, the introduction of a male to a female is, with caution, quite straightforward. Keep a watchful eye on the new couple, looking for signs of aggression from the female *(remove the male if necessary)*.

If interested, the female will present her rump to the male, offering him a brief period of mating. Once this has been successfully accomplished the male will devote himself to his mate, even giving up food for his partner. However, closer to the delivery date, she will become extremely aggressive, actively fending off her male partner. It is best to remove the male at this point, to prevent injury or even fatal wounding to the male or the female.

It is normally good breeding practice to introduce the female to the male in his cage. Leave her for around 15 minutes. The female is only in estrus (in season) for 12 hours so it can be difficult to time right. The best way to tell if a female is receptive is to place her with a male, if she is ready, she will present, If not she will fend the male off , so remove her and try again another day.

Top tips

Hamster pups

Hamster pups are born both hairless and with their eyes closed.

They begin to open their eyes around 4 to 6 days and their fur grows around this time also. They are totally dependant on their mother for sustenance at this time and only begin to eat solids along side their mothers milk at around 14 day. It is important to remove and sex the pups at 5 weeks as at the age of 6 weeks they become sexually capable and will begin to mate with their siblings.

Did you know?

Dwarf hamsters' breeding season is from April to September. But, if kept in lighting that stays on for eight hours or more a day, they will continue to breed throughout the entire year.

Titles in series

Copyright © 2012 Magnet & Steel Ltd
Publisher: Magnet & Steel Ltd

Magnet & Steel Ltd
Unit 6
Vale Business Park,
Llandow, United Kingdom. CF71 7PF
sales@magnetsteel.com
www.magnetsteel.com

ALL RIGHTS RESERVED
No parts of this book may be reproduced or transmitted in any form or by any means, electronic or mechanical, including photocopying, recording, or by any information storage and retrieval system, without permission in writing from the Publisher.

The advice contained in this book is provided as general information only. It does not relate to any specific case and should not be substituted for the advice or guidance of a licensed veterinary practitioner. Magnet & Steel Publishing Ltd do not accept liability or responsibility for any consequences resulting from the use of or reliance upon the information contained herein. No animal was harmed in the making of this book.